Pebble® Bilingüe/Bilingual Plus

¿QUÉ HAY EN MiPlato?

MERiENDAS SALUDABLES en MiPlato

HEALTHY SNACKS on MyPlate

WHAT'S ON MyPlate?

por/by Mari Schuh

Editora consultora/Consulting Editor:
Gail Saunders-Smith, PhD

Consultora/Consultant: Barbara J. Rolls, PhD
Guthrie Chair en Nutrición/Guthrie Chair in Nutrition
Pennsylvania State University
University Park, Pennsylvania

CAPSTONE PRESS
a capstone imprint

Pebble Plus is published by Capstone Press,
1710 Roe Crest Drive, North Mankato, Minnesota 56003
www.capstonepub.com

Library of Congress Cataloging-in-Publication Data
Schuh, Mari C., 1975– author.
  Meriendas saludables en MiPlato= Healthy snacks on MyPlate/ por Mari Schuh ; editora consultora, Gail Saunders-
Smith, PhD.
    pages cm. — (Pebble plus bilingüe. ¿Qué hay en miplato? = Pebble plus bilingual. What's on Myplate?)
  Spanish and English.
  Audience: K to grade 3
  Includes index.
  ISBN 978-1-62065-947-2 (library binding)
  ISBN 978-1-4765-1764-3 (ebook PDF)
1. Snack foods—Juvenile literature. 2. Nutrition—Juvenile literature. I. Saunders-Smith, Gail, editor. II. Schuh, Mari
C., 1975– Healthy snacks. Spanish. III. Schuh, Mari C., 1975– Healthy snacks. IV. Title. V. Title: Healthy snacks.
TX740.S325718 2013
642—dc23   2012022673

Summary: Simple text and photos describe USDA's MyPlate tool and its healthy snack choices
for children—in both English and Spanish

Editorial Credits
Jeni Wittrock, editor; Strictly Spanish, translation services; Gene Bentdahl, designer; Eric Manske, bilingual book
designer; Svetlana Zhurkin, media researcher; Jennifer Walker, production specialist; Sarah Schuette, photo stylist;
Marcy Morin, studio scheduler

Photo Credits
All photos by Capstone Studio/Karon Dubke except:
Shutterstock: Robyn Mackenzie, back cover, Svetlana Lukienko, cover; USDA, cover (inset), 7

Information in this book supports
the U.S. Department of Agriculture's
MyPlate food guidance system found at
www.choosemyplate.gov. Food amounts
listed in this book are based on daily
recommendations for children ages 4-8.
The amounts listed in this book are
appropriate for children who get less than
30 minutes a day of moderate physical
activity, beyond normal daily activities.
Children who are more physically active
may be able to eat more while staying
within calorie needs. The U.S. Department
of Agriculture (USDA) does not endorse
any products, services, or organizations.

Note to Parents and Teachers

The ¿Qué hay en MiPlato? /What's on MyPlate? series supports national science standards
related to health and nutrition. This book describes and illustrates healthy snacks, as
recommended by the USDA's MyPlate guidelines. The images support early readers in
understanding the text. The repetition of words and phrases helps early readers learn new
words. This book also introduces early readers to subject-specific vocabulary words, which are
defined in the Glossary section. Early readers may need assistance to read some words and to
use the Table of Contents, Glossary, Internet Sites, and Index sections of the book.

Printed in China.
092012   006934LEOS13

Table of Contents

Tabla de contenidos

Tasty Snacks/
Meriendas sabrosas

A snack is a small amount
of food you eat between meals.
The right snacks give you
energy until your next meal.

Una merienda es una pequeña cantidad
de alimento que comes entre comidas.
Las meriendas adecuadas te dan
energía hasta tu próxima comida.

MyPlate/ MiPlato

MyPlate is a tool that
helps you eat well.
MyPlate shows you how
to choose healthy foods.

MiPlato es una herramienta que
te ayuda a comer bien.
MiPlato te muestra cómo
seleccionar alimentos saludables.

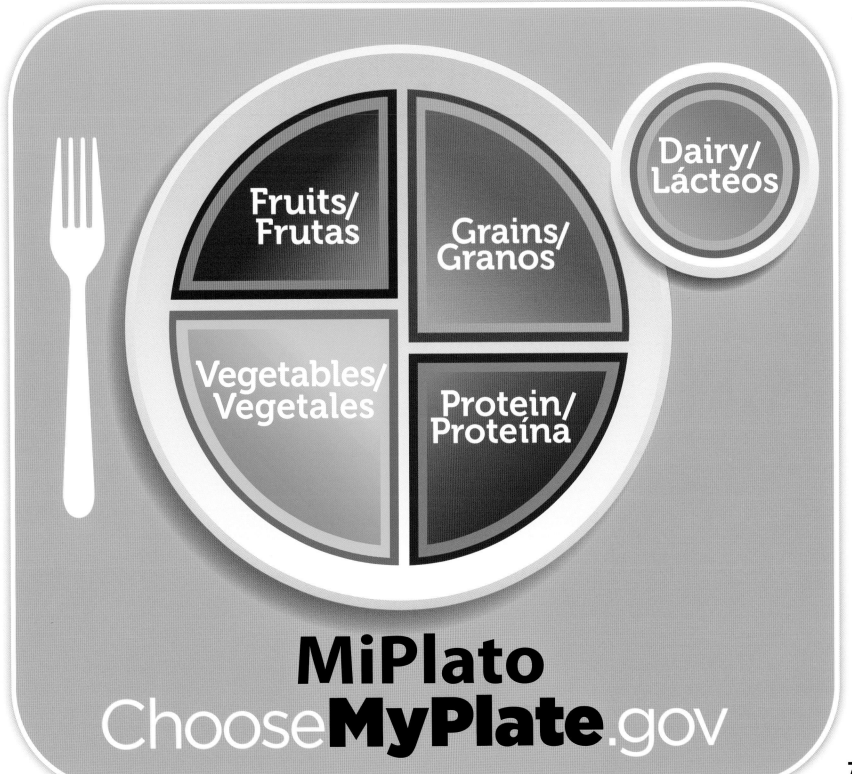

You can choose small snacks
from every food group.
Try to eat snacks made from
two or more food groups.

Puedes seleccionar pequeñas meriendas
de cada grupo de alimentos.
Trata de comer meriendas de dos
o más grupos de alimentos.

Snack Time/
Hora de la merienda

The best snacks taste good
and are good for you.
Graham crackers dipped in yogurt
are a healthful, yummy choice!

Las mejores meriendas tienen un sabor
rico y son buenas para ti.
La galletas Graham mojadas en yogur son
saludables y juna selección muy rica!

Can't wait until lunch?

A small peanut butter and banana sandwich

will keep you going until your next meal.

¿No puedes esperar hasta el almuerzo?

Un sándwich de mantequilla de

maní y bananas te dará energía

hasta tu próxima comida.

Rumble, rumble.

Is your stomach growling?

Make your own snack mix.

Choose cereal, nuts, seeds, and dried fruit.

Ruge, ruge.

¿Está rugiendo tu estómago?

Haz tu propia mezcla para la merienda.

Selecciona cereal, nueces, semillas y fruta seca.

Munch on crunchy veggies with
low-fat dip or salad dressing.
How many colors can you eat?

Come vegetales crujientes con dip o aderezo
para ensaladas bajos en grasas.
¿Cuántos colores puedes comer?

In a rush?

Fruit is a quick, healthy snack

that's easy to pack.

Grab an apple and go!

¿No tienes tiempo?

La fruta es una merienda rápida y

saludable que es fácil de empacar.

¡Toma una manzana y listo!

Tasty Snack Ideas/
Ideas de meriendas sabrosas

If you have the munchies between meals,

eat a small, healthy snack.

Small snacks will fuel your body

until your next meal.

Si tienes hambre entre comidas, come

meriendas pequeñas y saludables.

Las meriendas pequeñas le darán energía a tu

cuerpo hasta la próxima comida.

½ ounce (15 grams) sunflower seeds

½ onza (15 gramos) de semillas de girasol

carrots and low-fat dip

zanahorias y dip bajo en grasas

low-fat cheese and whole grain crackers

queso bajo en grasas y galletas integrales

orange slices

rodajas de naranja

mini rice cakes

galletas mini de arroz

½ cup (120 mL) cherry tomatoes

½ taza (120 ml) de tomates uva

sliced lean chicken with low-fat cheese

pollo magro en rebanadas con queso bajo en grasas

cereal with fruit

cereal con fruta

dried apricots

albaricoques secos

Glossary

energy—the strength to be active without getting tired

food group—one of the six different categories of foods people need, including dairy, fruit, grain, protein, sugars and fats, and vegetables

fuel—to give energy

MyPlate—a food plan that reminds people to eat healthful food and be active; MyPlate was created by the U.S. Department of Agriculture

snack—a small amount of food people eat between meals

Internet Sites

FactHound offers a safe, fun way to find Internet sites related to this book. All of the sites on FactHound have been researched by our staff.

Here's all you do:

Visit *www.facthound.com*

Type in this code: 9781620659472

Super-cool stuff! Check out projects, games and lots more at **www.capstonekids.com**

Glosario

la energía—la fuerza para estar activo sin cansarse

energizado—con energía

el grupo de alimentos—una de las seis diferentes categorías de alimentos que las personas necesitan, incluyendo lácteos, frutas, granos, proteínas, azúcares y grasas, y vegetales

la merienda—una pequeña cantidad de alimento que la gente come entre comidas

MiPlato—un plan de alimentos que hace recordar a la gente de comer alimentos saludables y de estar activos; MiPlato fue creado por el Departamento de Agricultura de EE.UU.

Sitios de Internet

FactHound brinda una forma segura y divertida de encontrar sitios de Internet relacionados con este libro. Todos los sitios en FactHound han sido investigados por nuestro personal.

Esto es todo lo que tienes que hacer:

Visita *www.facthound.com*

Ingresa este código: 9781620659472

¡Algo súper divertido! Hay proyectos, juegos y mucho más en **www.capstonekids.com**

Index

Índice